# Where's Jesus?

Written by Joe Ptak
Illustrated by Audrey Lemcool

Where's Jesus.
© 2024 by Joe Ptak
Illustrated by Audrey Lemcool



Printed in the United States of America.
ISBN-13: 979-8-218-35255-4 Paperback
979-8-218-35256-1 Hardcover
Library of Congress Control Number: 2024900988

Luke Lorraine Publishing
Indian Harbor Beach, Florida

To my amazing family, Jesus <u>is</u> everywhere!

Where's Jesus...?
He's with you on
your journey!

# Where's Jesus...?

He's helping you be safe!

Where's Jesus...?
He's helping us find
the best ingredients!
SALT

Where's Jesus...?
JESUS ♥ YOU
He's guiding your choices!

Where's Jesus…?
He's reminding us
to be thankful!

Where's Jesus..?
He's helping us have fun!

Where's Jesus...?
He's watching you soar!

Where's Jesus...?
He's sharing in the greatest gift!
HOLY BIBLE

# Where's Jesus...?

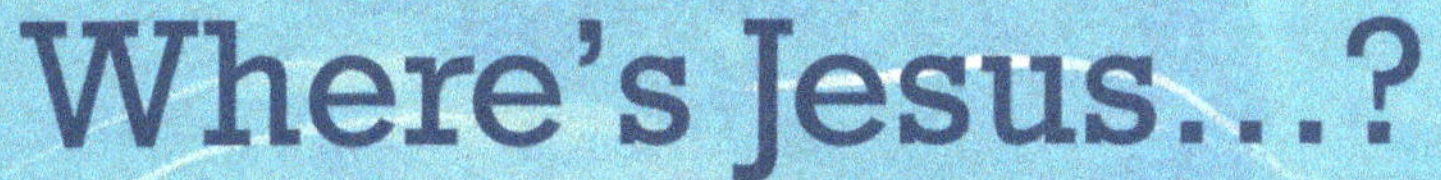

He's calming the
waters in your life!

Where's Jesus..?
Helping those less fortunate!
FOOD BANK

# Where's Jesus..?
## Helping you learn the facts!

Where's Jesus..?
Having fun along side you!

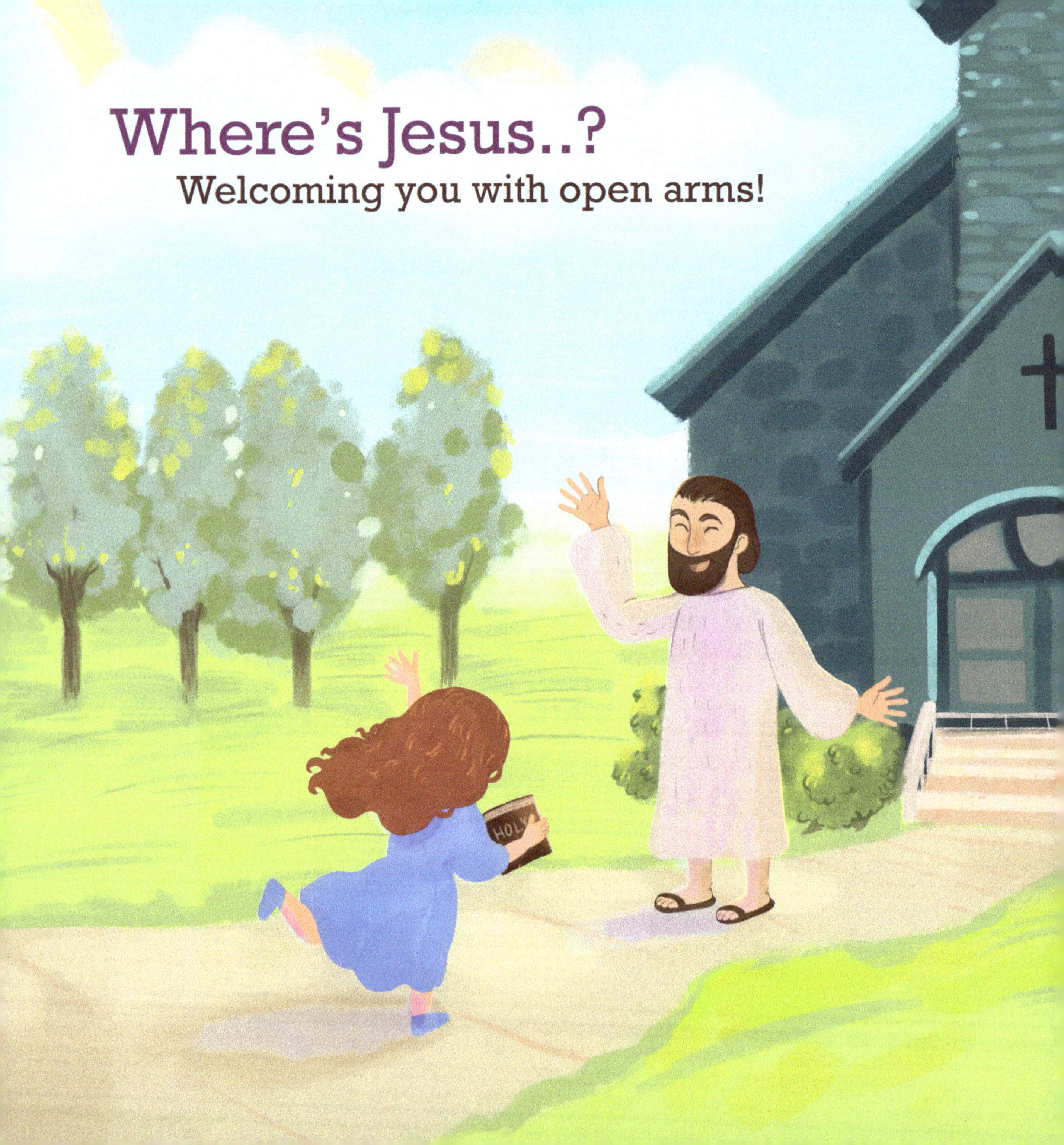
Where's Jesus..?
Welcoming you with open arms!
HOLY

Where's Jesus..?
Keeping you afloat when
you need it most!

Where's Jesus…?
He's welcoming
new life!

# Where's Jesus…?
## He's everywhere!